CW00960383

Wordsworth House and Garden

Cockermouth

National Trust

At Blindmans buff a Ball is enough

Childhood in the 18th century

During the 18th century, attitudes to children changed. Theorists such as Locke and Rousseau advised parents that children should not be cosseted and restricted, as they had been in previous centuries. Instead, they should be allowed to behave naturally and to play in the open air.

Mr and Mrs Wordsworth may have adopted this approach to bringing up their children. Mrs Wordsworth seems to have been close to her children. Indeed, William later described her as 'the heart and hinge of all our learnings and our loves'. He also remembers time spent reading with his father.

In spite of the new attitude to children, by today's standards discipline was strict. A difficult child with a 'stiff and moody and violent temper', William was regularly and severely punished for bad behaviour.

A POET'S BIRTHPLACE

'Fair seed-time had my soul, and I grew up
Foster'd alike by beauty and by fear;
Much favour'd in my birthplace ...'
THE PRELUDE (1805)

In 1764 John Wordsworth, a 23-year-old lawyer, moved into what is now called Wordsworth House. This was a 'tied' house, which came with his job as Agent for Sir James Lowther's Cumberland estates. For nearly twenty years it served as both his office and his family home.

John and Ann Wordsworth, who married in 1766, had five children, of whom William, the future poet, was the second. Richard was born in 1768, William in 1770, Dorothy on Christmas Day 1771, John in 1772 and Christopher in 1774. For many years their home must have echoed with the sounds of lively children. In poems written later, such as *The Prelude*, William Wordsworth recalls his early childhood in Cockermouth with warmth and happiness.

This happy life came to an end in 1778, when Ann Wordsworth died, aged only 30. Dorothy was sent to live with relatives in Halifax, while Richard and William left to attend Hawkshead Grammar School, returning to Cockermouth only in school holidays. Five years later, the children's lives were blighted further by the death of their father. At this point, they were forced into the care of relatives, leaving Cockermouth for ever.

Although sadly shortened, there is little doubt that William Wordsworth's early years in Cockermouth were extremely important to him. This was where he and Dorothy nurtured a devotion to the natural beauty of the Cumbrian countryside, which would inspire them for the rest of their lives.

During 2004 Wordsworth House was transformed by the National Trust in an exciting restoration project, to look as it might have when the Wordsworths lived here. Today, we hope you will get a tangible sense of what it was like to live in 18th-century Cockermouth.

Top The young William and Dorothy loved to play in the garden of Wordsworth House

Left William Wordsworth in 1798; the first reliable portrait

Opposite Toys in the Children's Bedroom include a jumping jack, wooden pull-along animals, building blocks, spinning tops, animals on sticks, a doll and a windmill

A CHANGING HOUSE

Above Robinson Mitchell who lived in the house from 1885 to 1907, and is thought to have introduced a lawn to the rear garden. He probably also added the main steps up to the terrace, on which he is photographed here

Opposite The front of the house is rendered in lime and finished in terracotta-coloured limewash. The slight staining from the run-off of the stone sills is a natural feature and is how it would have looked in the 18th century – frequent repainting would not have been practical. Evidence for the present colour was found under the eaves

Wordsworth House was built to impress. Its grand scale would have made quite an impact among the people of Cockermouth when it was first built at the end of the 17th century. The addition of a classical porch and the installation of Georgian sashes to the windows in the 1740s reaffirmed its status as the finest house in town.

The front garden has been laid out in recent times following archaeological research into what it might have looked like in the 18th century. This is a courtyard garden typical of the age, designed to show the status of the owner and make the best impression on visitors and passers-by. The two circular flowerbeds are surrounded by local red-sandstone flags and there are clipped box balls on either side of the gate. The formal effect is softened by herbs and perennials including roses, foxgloves, poppies, geraniums and iris.

Origins
Despite an inscription over the back door claiming that this house was built by Joshua Lucock in 1745, deeds show that the first owner was one William Bird in the 1690s.

The early 18th century
For the first 40 years of the 18th century, the house was lived in by agents to wealthy landowners, who seem to have altered it little. The first changes were made in 1744, when Joshua Lucock bought it for £350.

As Sheriff of Cumberland, Lucock was a man of considerable standing, which he wanted his house to reflect. During two years of improvements, he added decorative woodwork and plasterwork to the interior in a rich classical style, as well as fashionable new sash windows and a porch.

1764–83: John Wordsworth
By the 1760s, the house had passed into the hands of Sir James Lowther, whose agent, John Wordsworth, may at first have contented himself with refreshing the existing decoration. However, there is evidence that in about 1780 he updated the fireplaces by adding some elegantly carved overmantels.

The 19th century
During the 19th century few changes were made to the house. It remained in the hands of the Lowther family and was lived in by lawyers representing their interests – first James Clark Satterthwaite and then William Wood. In 1885 it was bought by Robinson Mitchell, an auctioneer, who sensitively improved the house and garden.

From doctor's surgery to poet's memorial
In 1937, after 30 years as a doctor's home and surgery, GP Edward Ellis agreed to sell the house to Cumberland Motor Services to make way for a bus station. A group of townspeople formed the Wordsworth Memorial Committee and raised £1,625 to buy the house. It was handed over to the National Trust in 1938 and had its official opening on 3 June 1939.

Above The design of a
Scotch double cloth carpet
of 1765 from Townend,
Troutbeck, was copied for
the Brussels Wilton carpet
in the Entrance Hall

Right The Front Office,
where John Wordsworth
would have carried out his
work as Agent to Sir James
Lowther, as well as his own
private legal practice with
other clients

A LIVING, WORKING HOME

The Entrance Hall ✎

With its fluted columns and impressive staircase, the hall was designed to make an impact on visitors. However, only the most important guests would have entered here. Most people had to use the rear entrance.

Clients or tenants waiting to see John Wordsworth might have been asked to sit in the hall. The bench has been made in Cumbrian oak, copying an 18th-century north-country original.

The Front Office ✎

This room is shown as the domain of John Wordsworth. One of the smartest rooms in the house, with fine panelling and an elaborate cornice, it may well have served as the 'Front Office' mentioned in Wordsworth family papers.

Furniture

The mahogany desk, on loan from the Wordsworth Trust, is known to have belonged to John Wordsworth and may have been made for this room. It is dated 1766 – the year in which he married Ann Cookson. On the desk are copies of some of the letters and other documents written here by John Wordsworth.

Prints

After John Wordsworth's death in 1783, a notice appeared in *The Cumberland Pacquet* newspaper, advertising the sale of his belongings (illustrated on p.27). Included in the list of items for sale was 'a great Variety of valuable Prints, glassed and framed'. The prints on the walls here reflect the type of image likely to have been collected by Mr Wordsworth. Either side of the desk are portrait engravings of the reigning monarch, King George III, and Queen Charlotte. There are also two 18th-century coloured maps of Cumberland and Westmorland, including one dated 1760, which is dedicated to Sir James Lowther (right of fireplace).

Sir James Lowther

Sir James Lowther (1736–1802) was one of the wealthiest and most powerful men in 18th-century England. He inherited a massive fortune and vast estates, including the Whitehaven collieries, at the age of fourteen. In 1761 he married Lady Mary Stuart, whose father became Prime Minister the following year. He was made 1st Earl of Lonsdale in 1784.

Lowther's ambition was to control all ten parliamentary seats in Cumberland and Westmorland. They included Cockermouth, where Lowther spent £58,060 in 1756 acquiring a majority of the 278 burgages in the town. Ownership of these plots of land brought with it the right to nominate Cockermouth's two MPs without an election. During the second half of the 18th century, Lowther dominated the political life of the region.

Above Sir James Lowther was renowned for being ruthless, determined and mean. He was widely detested and feared by people in the area, earning the nickname 'the Tyrant of the North'

The Dining Room ✎

This would have been one of the Wordsworths' best rooms, used for dinner parties and family meals on special occasions.

Plasterwork

This is the only room in the house to have decorative plasterwork on the ceiling, which gives the room a higher status. The evidence of paint analysis shows that most of the decoration dates from 1744–6. The fire surround was updated at the same time, although the late 18th-century decorative overmantel may have been added by John Wordsworth.

Furnishings

The furniture, such as the mahogany Hepplewhite chairs, is typical of a middle-class Georgian dining room, as is the mid-green paint colour. There are no curtains, because soft furnishings were thought to harbour the smell of stale food.

The Back Office ✎

John Wordsworth employed a clerk to assist him in administering Lowther's Cumberland estates. This simple room, located conveniently close to the Front Office, may have served as his office. Here, the clerk would have laboured for long hours, keeping records, copying documents and receiving tenants.

Tools of the trade

Among the scattered papers are items likely to have been used every day by a clerk, such as a wax-jack (a self-snuffing candle), ink pots and bottles, quills and coins. Estate maps hang on the walls, including a reproduction of Thomas Donald's 1774 map of Cumberland.

An agent's life

John Wordsworth's job as Agent involved travelling around Lowther's Cumberland estates holding manor courts (which arbitrated on local disputes), collecting rents from tenants and inspecting estate properties. He also defended his master in legal matters and became involved in canvassing political support for him at election time. His salary was £100 a year.

Wordsworth's accounts show that he was an extremely busy man, often away from home on Lowther business and travelling long distances on horseback. A recently discovered day book has revealed that he also had his own private legal practice, which seems to have been lucrative.

Top John Wordsworth employed at least one clerk in the Back Office. One man, William Arnott, stayed with him for ten years, and was paid £5 per quarter

Above The furniture in the Back Office, including a desk and stool in elm and a pine plan chest, has been remade following 18th-century office furniture shown in pictures such as *The Cabinet Maker's Office*

Above The oak dresser in the Common Parlour is laden with crockery that the family would have used on a daily basis: creamware plates and jugs, pewter dishes and tankards, salt and pepper pots, and a collection of wine glasses

Right A recipe from Elizabeth Raffald's *Experienced English Housekeeper* (1775)

Opposite The Kitchen is the heart of the home, and cluttered with reproduction and antique cooking utensils. The kettle is always on and apple rings dry in the heat

Opposite far right Earthenware and stoneware jars, filled with grain, flour, dried fruits, herbs and spices, and sealed with chamois leather

The Common Parlour ✎

A common parlour was a multi-purpose room, likely to have been used regularly by the family, and often serving as a dining room. Mrs Wordsworth may have worked in here during the day, while keeping an eye on the maid in the Kitchen next door.

Furniture

As this would not have been one of the Wordsworths' best rooms, it may have housed their more old-fashioned oak furniture. In this room the collection of antique furniture includes the kind of pieces commonly found in mid-18th-century households in the north of England. The oak mule chest was made for Thomas Iredale of Cockermouth in 1737, and many of the chairs come from the Lake District.

The Kitchen ✎

The Wordsworths' kitchen would have been at the heart of their home – a centre of activity, a source of noise, warmth and smells, and a place for the servants and children to eat. But a room like this must have been a tiring environment in which to work.

This fascinating room has been recreated by food historian Peter Brears, based on evidence found in the room and examples of similar kitchens elsewhere.

Fixtures and fittings

In Georgian times, the most important cooking methods were roasting, boiling and stewing. In this kitchen, roasting would have taken place on a spit in front of a fire burning in the cast-iron range. The spit would have been turned by a smoke-jack fitted to the chimneybreast, powered by the passage of hot air upwards through the flue. A wood-fired 'beehive' oven, fitted to the right of the range, would have been used for baking bread and cakes. The range is flanked by a boiling copper (on the right) and a charcoal stewing stove (on the left) used for making sauces.

In the corner, by the boiling copper, the sink is fitted with a draining rack. Next to it is a dresser with a 'delft rack' above, for storing plates. Opposite the fireplace, an arched recess has been fitted out as a built-in dresser – the shelves loaded with pots, pans and jars.

Furniture

The large centre table is a replica of a traditional kitchen table which provides a surface for preparing vegetables, rolling pastry, beating eggs and stirring cake mixture. Its sycamore top can be scrubbed down at the end of the day. A replica dough trough, in which dough was mixed, fermented and left to prove before baking, stands between the windows.

To make a rich Seed Cake.

TAKE a Pound of Flour well dried, a Pound of Butter, a Pound of Loaf Sugar beat and sifted, eight Eggs, two Ounces of Carriway Seeds, one Nutmeg grated, and its Weight of Cinnamon; first beat your Butter to a Cream, then put in your Sugar, beat the Whites of your Eggs half an Hour, mix them with your Sugar and Butter, then beat the Yolks half an Hour, put it to the Whites, beat in your Flour, Spices, and Seeds, a little before it goes to the Oven, put it in the Hoop and bake it two Hours in a quick Oven, and let it stand two Hours.—It will take two Hours beating.

Food and drink

The food eaten by the Wordsworth household would have been plain and substantial. Meals would have been dominated by meat, fish, pies and dairy produce. Filled suet puddings and sweet baked puddings were also popular. A variety of vegetables, grown in the garden, would have been served boiled, often covered with melted butter. Apples, rhubarb and gooseberries were eaten raw, added to tarts or made into jams.

When cooking, it is very likely that Mrs Wordsworth and her maid worked from books such as Elizabeth Raffald's *Experienced English Housekeeper* (1775), in which they would have found recipes for 'pike boiled with a pudding in the belly', potted char (a local fish), 'calf's head surprise', herb fritters and syllabubs.

Top The Best Parlour wallpaper reproduces an English design of the 1760s. It is block-printed in distemper on small sections of paper – as it would have been in the 18th century

Above The advertisement listing items for sale after John Wordsworth's death includes 'a large and handsome Wilton Carpet', which was probably laid in the Drawing Room. This new Wilton was woven to the design of an 18th-century Indian carpet

Right The Best Parlour

Opposite The Drawing Room

The Best Parlour ✎

In this comfortable room, overlooking the garden, Mrs Wordsworth might have written letters at her desk or kept her accounts. This was a room containing some of the family's better mahogany furniture, where they could entertain close friends.

Furniture

The mahogany kneehole desk has been newly made following a *c.*1760 original by the Lancaster-based firm, Gillows, which produced some of the most fashionable furniture available in the 18th century. Such an elegant small-sized desk would have been used by the lady of the house, who would have been able to lock her papers in the drawers to prevent servants snooping at the contents!

Two fine chairs, also made new, have been fitted with blue check case covers over

upholstery of scarlet harateen (a woollen cloth often chosen for furnishings in the 18th century), which has also been used for the curtains.

The Wordsworth Room ✎

This contains a settee and longcase clock owned by Wordsworth in later life.

The Drawing Room ✎

This grand and imposing room was probably used only when Mr and Mrs Wordsworth were entertaining. Here they could show off their most fashionable furnishings. When not in use, the furniture would have been fitted with covers, to protect it from dust and children.

Decoration

Paint analysis has shown that, when the Wordsworths moved in, this room was probably painted an olive green colour, as it is now. This was the first colour applied to the panelling and carved decoration, installed in the 1740s.

Furniture

The furniture – arranged for a social occasion – includes a set of Chippendale armchairs of *c.*1755 upholstered in red wool damask, a set of early 18th-century walnut chairs with horsehair seats (which once belonged to the poet Robert Southey) and William Wordsworth's bureau bookcase of *c.*1780. The walnut-cased harpsichord is a working replica of one by William Smith of London, *c.*1720, which may have belonged to Handel.

Above Music formed an integral part of 18th-century social gatherings. If the family owned an instrument a harpsicord would have been the likeliest choice

Entertaining

As a prominent figure in Cockermouth, John Wordsworth may have played host to friends and business associates. The arrangements would have been made by his wife, anxious to provide an impressive display of food and drink.

After dinner, the ladies would retire to the Drawing Room, while the men raised toasts and drank more wine. Tea would be served for the entire party, who might then play cards or dance.

Top The Closet wallpaper is a replica of a 1760s pattern

Above The design of the Scotch double cloth carpet in the Children's Bedroom is the reverse of the one copied for the Entrance Hall

Right Mrs Wordsworth's Bedroom, with the Closet beyond

THE WORDSWORTHS' BEDROOMS

Leading directly off the landing, the best bedchamber, shown as Mrs Wordsworth's Bedroom, is a handsome panelled room with a closet. A second bedroom (Mr Wordsworth's) is approached through a connecting doorway.

Mrs Wordsworth's Bedroom 🖎

The room is dominated by a Chippendale-style four-poster bed, hung with white lawn linen with a floral sprig pattern. This fabric, copying an English fabric dating from 1765, is also used for the 18th-century-style 'festoon' window curtains. The mid-18th-century oak tripod table is thought to have belonged to Dorothy Wordsworth.

Pictures

The panelled walls are decorated with three embroidered silkwork pictures, an oil portrait – *Boy with a Bird's Nest* after the English artist Thomas Hudson – and an engraving of a Scottish ballad scene all dating from the 1760s or 1770s.

Gown

Laid out on the bed is a gown made of dark red silk taffeta which would have been worn by a woman of Mrs Wordsworth's standing. It is in the 'Polonaise' style of the 1770s.

The Closet 🖎

The Closet, papered with a replica 1760s wallpaper and border, was used as a dressing room. The 1770s chest of drawers belonged to the poet Robert Southey.

Mr Wordsworth's Bedroom 🖎

The bed has been newly made in the style of Gillows of Lancaster. The footposts – the only visible part of the bed frame – are African mahogany (from sustainable sources), whereas the rest is local oak. The bed-hangings and window curtains are blue harateen.

Around the bed is a simple arrangement of furniture which John Wordsworth might have collected in the 1760s and 1770s, although the walnut dressing table is early 18th century. The commode corner chair would have housed a chamber pot.

The Children's Bedroom 🖎

It is possible that all five Wordsworth children shared this large plain room at the back of the house. From here they would have been able to look out over their favourite playground – the garden and the banks of the River Derwent.

Furniture

Just as happens today, the Wordsworths would have relegated their old-fashioned furniture to rooms such as the Children's Bedroom. The painted pine clothes press, side-table and rocking chair have been made to reflect this kind of furniture. The early 18th-century oak bed came from Lancashire. It is strung with rope and cannot have been particularly comfortable.

Wicker cradles were popular during the Wordsworths' time, not only because they were light and airy, but also because they could be burnt easily in case of disease.

Toys and games

Today, most children have a vast array of exciting and colourful toys. Children in the 18th century, however, would have owned fewer, simpler toys. Most of those owned by the Wordsworth children would have been homemade, from wood or cloth. Some may have been bought from street traders at fairs and markets.

The first books written specifically for children were published in the 1740s, such as the *Little Pretty Pocket Book* by John Newbery, and soon a wide variety was available to buy. Magical fairy tales, handed down for generations, were also a common source of amusement.

Above The Children's Bedroom

15

THE GARDEN

Top The vibrant red of peonies adds drama to the side beds

Above The maid-of-all-work picks 'Greenup's Pippins' for the Kitchen

William Wordsworth's memories of his early life in Cockermouth are dominated by happy times spent exploring the garden. It was also a vital source of produce for the Wordsworth household.

A changing garden

The basic structure of the rear garden, with a smaller walled garden and a raised terrace running parallel to the River Derwent, dates from the 1690s when the house was built. A flight of steps from the main garden to the terrace was added in the 19th century.

In 2003, research including a geophysical survey, an archaeological dig, a study of local maps and a comparison with other town gardens of the period was undertaken to discover how the garden had been altered over the previous 300 years.

The following year, the central area of lawn was removed and replaced with vegetable plots surrounded by grass paths. Since then, it has been replanted as far as possible with plants from the 18th century.

The flood of November 2009 laid large areas of the garden to waste. This provided an opportunity to make it even more authentically Georgian. Vegetable and flower beds were realigned to create greater symmetry, and the grass paths replaced with gravel. A summerhouse, cold frames and trellising were erected, a new cut-flower area created and the range of 18th-century plants greatly increased.

The wall borders

Gravel paths lead between the wall borders and the physic beds. Oak trellising has been constructed according to the sorts of fruit planted against it, with rails six inches apart for fruit fans and espaliers and, in the small walled garden, nine inches apart for climbing plants. As Philip Miller wrote in *The Gardeners Dictionary* of 1768, 'Trellises may be made of any sort of timber, according to the expense which the owner is willing to bestow … but if any person will go to the expense of oak, it will last much longer.'

The east-facing wall borders (the left-hand wall looking towards the terrace) contain espaliered heritage varieties of pears 'William's Bon Cretien' (1760), 'Louis Bonne of Jersey' and 'Catillac', a culinary pear first recorded in 1665. Growing alongside them are a fig and a fan of Morello cherry.

On the west-facing (right-hand) walls grow 'Hawthornden', a very old Scottish cooking apple; 'Ribston Pippin' and the rare 'Acklam Russet', both Yorkshire apples from the 1700s.

Within low box hedging there are herbs and perennial flowers: day lilies, peonies, asters, Maltese cross, sweet woodruff, red hot pokers, lily of the valley and geraniums. Among the more prominent perennials are angelica, giant scabious and Joe Pye weed.

Under the south-facing terrace walls are plum fans – greengage, claimed to be the oldest plum or gage still in cultivation, and 'Mirabelle de Nancy' with its small yellow fruit.

The physic beds

The long beds running parallel with the wall borders are physic beds, for plants with medicinal uses.

'Greenup's Pippin' apples – a late 18th-century dual purpose Lancastrian variety – are underplanted with herbs, including pink and white flowering hyssop, bistort, tansy, feverfew, primrose and cowslip, as well as wild white strawberries and the highly scented roses 'Celsiana' and 'Alba Maxima', the white rose of York.

The rose bed

The end bed is planted with two Portugal quinces, whose fruit has a strong floral fragrance and resembles a cross between a pear and a golden apple, and varieties of old-fashioned shrub roses. These include 'Rosa Mundi', which has large pink, white and crimson blooms and is said to be named after Fair Rosamund, mistress of Henry II; the crimson rose of Lancaster, also known as the apothecary's rose, and 'Quatre Saisons', one of the oldest roses, which has an unusual second flush of flowers in late summer. The bed is edged with aromatic grey-green cat mint.

In spring, tulips – the unusual spidery red and yellow flowers of *Acuminata*, one of the oldest hybrids; the mildly fragrant scarlet-edged yellow blooms of *Tulipa Keizerskroon*, and the yellow buds of native *Sylvestris* – mingle with clumps of blue grape hyacinth.

Heritage varieties of tulips, daffodils and crocuses can be found throughout the garden in spring, including William's 'host of golden daffodils' *Narcissus pseudonarcissus lobularis* (Lent lily).

The cut-flower bed

The end bed nearest the house provides cut flowers such as asphodel, with grassy foliage and tall spiky yellow flowers; globe thistle, which has clear blue spheres; masterwort, with papery white flowers; Jacob's ladder, whose leaves resemble a series of rungs; the spires of blue speedwell, and cone flower, with big purple-red daisy flowers.

The cardoon bed

The triangular bed at the end of the cut-flower bed is dominated by a cardoon, which is similar to a giant artichoke and has spiny silver-grey leaves and large thistle-like purple flower heads. It is accompanied by aromatic wormwood, from whose root absinthe is extracted to make liqueur, and the bed is edged with the dark blue flowering form of hyssop.

Below right Stately spires of the common foxglove self-seed throughout the garden

Below The 12th-century *Rosa Mundi*

Left Ann Wordsworth leaves behind the stresses of caring for five small children and a bustling household to enjoy a tranquil stroll

Below The impressive flower head of the cardoon

Top The zesty orange of
the annual pot marigold

Above William and Dorothy
return to view the
summerhouse

The vegetable beds

The central vegetable plots are planted in a
potager style, with herbs and flowers mixed
with varieties of vegetables available in the
18th century. The gardener rotates these
each year to improve the fertility of the soil,
just as the Wordsworths' gardener might
have done. Annual flowers such as borage,
pot marigold, cornflower and sage are grown
with the vegetables to attract bees and
assist pollination.

Among the older and more unusual
vegetable varieties cultivated are black
Spanish long and round winter radishes,
purslane, orach, two forms of beetroot –
golden and 'Tonda di Choggia', which has
red and white striped flesh – and 'Giant
d'Italia' parsley, which resembles celery.

The brassica bed has old varieties of
cabbages and the cauliflower purple cape.

Two of the beds are permanently planted,
one with broad-leaved sorrel, horseradish,
good King Henry, salad burnet and Welsh
onions, and the other laid out to bushes of
gooseberries and red and white currants
interspersed with salad crops.

The last of the beds has runner bean
'Painted Lady' growing up ash poles with
two old varieties of sweet pea, 'Matacuna'
and 'Painted Lady'. Peas and nasturtiums
ramble over hazel sticks woven into a
tunnel, alongside asparagus peas and the
dwarf French bean 'Lazy Housewife'.

The terrace

The terrace would have been created as a
promenade on which to take exercise and view
the river. For William and Dorothy, however, it
was a favourite playground alive with birds
and butterflies. In *The Prelude*, he recalls many
hours spent on the terrace, and Dorothy writes
in her letters of its privet and roses.

Three types of rose scramble over the
terrace walls and weave between the privet
bushes: *Rosa arvensis*, which has single creamy
flowers and autumnal red hips; the burnet
rose (*Pimpinellifolia*) with masses of creamy
flowers followed by blackish hips, and the
common sweet briar rose (*Rubiginosa*) with its
soft pink flowers and later orange hips. Two
Dutch honeysuckles (*Belgica*) and (*Serotina*)
scent the air, and hellebores, geraniums,
Solomon's seal, double meadow sweet and
Martagon lilies tumble over the path.

At the west end is an oak Georgian-style
summerhouse. An oak bench allows visitors
to view the River Derwent while listening to
a selection of William's poetry on a wind-up
audio unit.

Although there is no evidence of a
summerhouse in the Wordsworths' time, an
1839 tithe map shows a small building on
this spot. There are also known to have been
wooden summerhouses on the terrace from
the early 19th to the mid-20th centuries.

Both Dove Cottage and Rydal Mount,
later homes of William and Dorothy, also had
rustic garden pavillions.

The poet William Cowper (1731–1800)
commented of his summerhouse: 'Here I
write all that I write in summer-time,
whether to the Public or to my friends. It is
secure from all noise, and a refuge from all
intrusions … A poet's retreat is sacred.'

Above The manservant
reads a selection of
William's poetry inspired
by his childhood in
Cockermouth

Left A scarecrow assists the
gardener in frightening off
the birds. The garden is
managed following organic
principles and is peat-free

Top A white-tailed bumblebee visits the blue flower head of a globe thistle

Above A garden volunteer feeds one of the Scots Dumpy hens

Right White blooms of *Rosa arvensis* frame the small walled garden

The small walled garden

From this garden, the original steps lead up to the terrace – the other set are a Victorian addition.

In the centre of the lawn are two rare apple trees, 'Red Ladies Finger', a cider apple, and 'Keswick Codlin', a 1790 Lancastrian variety said by Robert Hogg in *The Fruit Manual* (1884) to have been discovered 'growing among a quantity of rubbish behind a wall at Gleaston Castle near Ulverston'.

This area is surrounded by aromatic herbs including thyme, sweet cicely, rosemary, lemon balm and lovage, all used in the working Georgian kitchen. The walls are covered with various climbers. The east-facing wall is screened by a hop, which apart from its use in beer, could be harvested in April as an asparagus substitute. The protected sunny lower terrace wall supports a Gagarin blue grape.

On the west-facing wall, roses 'Janet B. Wood' (1768) with its creamy white blooms and 'Blush Noisette' (18th century), said to be one of the earliest noisettes, mingle with the small purple bells of *Clematis viticella*, which dates from the 16th century.

In the bed below, the deep crimson bordering on purple flowers of the velvet rose *Rosa Tuscany* (pre 1596) are offset by the silvery leaves of southernwood and wormwood and the feathery foliage of bronze fennel.

The small cut-flower bed

The small cut-flower bed has been planted with choice 18th-century flowers including asters, campanulas, phloxes, thalictrums and rudbeckias to grace the best rooms in the house. It is edged with varieties of heritage dianthus.

Growing by the wall is the little-known 16th-century small black bullace, a relative of the plum, with a bitter fruit that can be used in jams.

Two oak cold frames enable the gardener to start off herbs, vegetables and annual flowers.

The hen house and enclosure

Records indicate the Wordsworths kept hens. Our Georgian-style hen house and enclosure are in the small walled garden to hide them from view of the house. The design, using hand-made nails and surrounded by a split oak palisade, is based on woodcuts of rural life by Thomas Bewick (1753–1828).

We keep a small flock of Scots Dumpy hens to provide eggs for the working kitchen.

Top 'Red Ladies Finger' cider apples

Above A terracotta pot of crocuses sits on the steps leading to the terrace

Left Cone Flower (*Echinacea Purpurea*)

DAILY LIFE IN THE WORDSWORTHS' HOME

The Wordsworths were a middle-class family, living in a grand and spacious house. Relative to most other people in Cockermouth, they appear to have led a comfortable existence.

Above Paintings such as this anonymous conversation-piece show how simply middle-class homes like Wordsworth House were decorated and furnished in the mid-18th century

Opposite Mr Wordsworth's Bedroom

Below Mr Wordsworth's account book provides much detail about the servants he employed

Organising the housework

As mistress of the house, the young Ann Wordsworth would have overseen the running of the household. She probably relied for advice on such household manuals as Martha Bradley's *The British Housewife* and *The Servant's Directory* by Hannah Glasse, which provided encyclopaedic instruction in successful housekeeping.

The Wordsworths' servants

The Wordsworths employed a modest, but standard, range of servants, including a maid-of-all-work, a manservant, a nurse to care for the children, and a 'jobbing' gardener.

The lot of the maid-of-all-work was by far the hardest, with most of the housekeeping chores falling to her. Records show that one girl, Amy, worked for the family for some time. Starting the day early, she would have cleaned grates, laid fires, emptied chamber-pots, washed floors, brushed carpets, dusted and tidied rooms, and aired and made beds. In addition, she would have cooked and prepared meals and probably washed up afterwards. At least one day of her week would have been devoted to laundering the family's dirty linen.

By comparison, the manservant had far less to do. Despite this, Mr Wordsworth's accounts show that he had difficulty filling this position, recording payments to a succession of troublesome individuals, one of whom appears to have robbed him. Nevertheless, the manservant was probably trusted with jobs requiring more skill, such as cleaning chandeliers or silver plate. He may also have cleaned the stables and looked after his master's horses. In the afternoon he would have changed into his livery, to act as footman to his master.

Lighting the home

The Wordsworths' house would have been lit by candles, probably arranged by the manservant. As candles were expensive and burnt quickly, they were lit only when a room was in use. Tallow candles (made from rendered animal fat) would have been used most frequently, even though they smelt unpleasant. Wax candles were reserved for special occasions.

Above An 18th-century kitchen, illustrated in Martha Bradley's *The British Housewife* (1756)

Above Much of the furniture
has been remade following
historic patterns

Right The garden after
the 2004 refurbishment.
Following the flood of 2009,
the beds were realigned and
the grass paths replaced by
more authentic gravel

RESTORING WORDSWORTH HOUSE

Research

Before recent times, comparatively little was known about the history of Wordsworth House or the people who once lived here, so a thorough programme of research was carried out before any changes were made. Architectural historians were called in to determine how the house had been altered over the centuries, while archivists searched census returns and other records at local record offices to trace past occupants.

The household accounts (at Dove Cottage, Grasmere) provided clear information about the Wordsworths' way of life, such as who they employed as servants, where they shopped and what they bought. The local newspaper, *The Cumberland Pacquet*, revealed fascinating facts about life in 1770s Cockermouth, and a study of inventories began to show how they might have furnished their house.

Decoration

Paint analysts examined samples from almost every painted surface to provide an insight into how the Wordsworths might have decorated their house. Today, the paint colours in most rooms show the results of this investigation. The types of paint used (such as casein distempers) were chosen to give the finish and texture characteristic of an 18th-century home.

Furnishings

A house becomes a home only once it is full of the belongings of the people who live there. The challenge at Wordsworth House has been to find pieces likely to have been owned by families of middling status like the Wordsworths, and, where possible, originating from Cumbria. Today, the 'best' rooms (at the front of the house) have been furnished with antiques dating from the mid- to late 18th century, collected over several years.

Furnishings for the informal 'hands-on' rooms have been made by specialist craftspeople and conservators, replicating 18th-century examples. Great efforts have been made to use traditional techniques and materials, so that the finished products look and feel as they did in the 1770s. Replica items include furniture crafted by cabinetmakers and utensils forged by blacksmiths.

As good as new
Many of the replica items seem unexpectedly new and brightly coloured. This is because the aim throughout has been to present the house as it was lived in by the Wordsworths – when many things around them would have been new.

Below This advertisement, which appeared in *The Cumberland Pacquet*, lists some of the items we know to have once been in Wordsworth House

HOUSEHOLD FURNITURE for SALE.

Cockermouth, April 17, 1784.

THE Sale of the valuable Household Goods & Furniture, late of Mr. JOHN WORDSWORTH, of Cockermouth, will begin on Wednesday the 5th Day of May next, at Ten o'Clock in the Forenoon, and continue till the Whole be Sold: the same consist of Plate, China, very good Beds, Bed and Table Linen, Mahogany Bed Stocks, Tables and Chairs, handsome oval and square Looking Glasses, a large and handsome Wilton Carpet, a great Variety of valuable Prints, glassed and framed, and all other useful Household Utensils.

The Housekeeper will shew the Goods to any Person desirous to see them before the Sale.

All Persons who stood indebted to the late Mr. John Wordsworth, at the Time of his Decease, are required to pay their respective Debts immediately to the Administrators, or to Mr. RICHARD WORDSWORTH, Attorney at Law, at Branthwaite, near Whitehaven. (16)

THE GREAT FLOOD OF 2009

Below Water from the River Derwent begins to fill the back garden

Bottom Ruined shop stock in the cellars after the flood waters receded

Opposite At its height, the flood water reached almost to the top of the house steps

Cockermouth's position at the point where the River Cocker flows into the Derwent is the key to its historic prosperity and its vulnerability. In the Wordsworths' time, the town bustled with millers, tanners, spinners, weavers and dyers, who relied on the plentiful water supply. Like residents before and after them, they lived with the threat of flooding.

On Thursday, 19 November 2009, the rain gauge at Seathwaite, in nearby Borrowdale, registered more than 300mm in 24 hours – a UK record. Wordsworth House was closed for the winter, but its shop was still open. By mid-morning the bottom of the garden had started to flood. By early afternoon, mini geysers were spurting through the cellar wall and the shop was awash.

Forced to leave

In no time at all, Main Street was a raging torrent and the cellar thigh deep. Having salvaged what they could from the shop, staff and volunteers carried John Wordsworth's desk and the mahogany Hepplewhite dining chairs upstairs before reluctantly abandoning the house on police instructions.

By early evening, the water was close to three metres deep in some streets and flowing at up to 25mph. Hundreds of people had abandoned their homes and businesses, but more than 500 were trapped. The emergency services, armed forces, Mountain Rescue, RNLI and Coastguard combed the streets by boat and helicopter, plucking people from windows and roofs.

Devastation and a miracle

Miraculously, less than 48 hours after it had arrived, the flood water was gone, and on Monday morning, the police allowed people back into the town centre. There was a scene of devastation: part of the front garden wall was gone and the massive wooden gates had been ripped from their fixings and carried off. The shop was a wreck and the front courtyard almost impassable with debris. Visitor reception and the washhouse were little better.

In the garden, walls were down, plants had been ripped out by the roots, and the tree-lined terrace where William and Dorothy played lay open to the river.

The rushing water had woven brightly coloured wool in intricate patterns around trees and bushes, and dumped booty from shops and homes, including DVDs, chocolate bars, toys and baby clothes, and even a small chest of drawers and a wicker linen basket.

Back in business

Bolstered by messages of support and offers of help from around the world, staff and volunteers set to work. They sluiced away tonnes of mud, removed barrow-loads of silt and filled sacks with debris.

Weeks of stripping out, emptying dehumidifiers, building work and refitting followed. On Saturday, 13 March, the last panel was put in place in the revamped visitor reception. Nine hours later, Wordsworth House and Garden reopened for its 2010 season, exactly on schedule.

THE CELLARS

The cellars at Wordsworth House face north, helping keep them cool for storing food and drink. There are three distinct areas, which would have been a dairy, a wine and beer cellar, and a larder. Before the 2009 flood, they were used for storage. After the flood, they were cleared completely to allow further investigation of how they were arranged. The areas that housed the dairy and wine and beer cellar are not on the visitor route, but we have now recreated the larder as it was in the Wordsworths' time.

The dairy

William's father John kept a cow in a field across the River Derwent. The maid would walk over the bridge every day with her stool and a pail known as a 'kit' to do the milking. She would bring the contents of her kit back to the east cellar (on the left of the illustration opposite), which is currently used as a storeroom.

It had a single, external door, now bricked up – the door connecting it to the other cellars is a later addition. The dairy's walls are still lined with 18th-century stone benches. A ventilation grille in the back wall helps keep the temperature low enough to make and store butter, curds and cheese.

The wine and beer cellar

The middle cellar was used for wine and beer, and could be accessed only from the west cellar, which was the larder. There would have been a strong, locked door between the two, to keep the precious bottles and barrels safe. The wine and beer cellar also had an inner, timber screen with a second locked door to provide additional security. The sockets for this can still be seen in the floor.

Only Mr Wordsworth and his most trusted servant would have had a key to this – they could choose wines and leave them in the vestibule between the doors for collection by another servant later in the day.

The larder

This was in the area closest to the back door (on the right of the illustration), making it convenient for deliveries and for the kitchen. Grilles leading to the space under the front rooms ensured the air remained cool.

More substantial Georgian houses had separate larders for raw and cooked meats, but Wordsworth House had just one. The room had a range of stone benches, a wooden safe for perishable foods, a shelf occupying its southern wall and a free-standing stone table in the centre of the floor.

Below left After the 2009 flood, the cellars were turned into a temporary exhibition space. Prince Charles, the National Trust's president, visited in 2010

Below When the terrace was damaged in the 2009 flood, a large dump of 17th and 18th-century pottery was found. We used these finds to make accurate replacement items for the restored larder

INSPIRING THE POET

'A sort of national property, in which every man has a right and interest who has an eye to perceive and a heart to enjoy.'
WORDSWORTH
on the Lake District

Below Crummock Water in the Buttermere valley. In later life, Wordsworth's passion for the Cumbrian countryside would inspire not only his poetry, but also a fierce commitment to protect the Lake District from inappropriate development – a philosophy at the heart of the National Trust's work in the area today

'The Child is father of the Man.'
TO A RAINBOW

Although William was just thirteen when his father died, five years after his mother, he remembered his parents with strong affection. Of his mother he recalled tenderness, piety and wisdom. From his father he learnt an appreciation of literature – a love for what he later referred to as his 'golden store of books'.

The death of Mr and Mrs Wordsworth left their children 'destitute, and as we might Trooping together'. Their situation worsened when Sir James Lowther refused to pay them £4,625 owed to their father in expenses (£250,000 today). This dispute, centring on Lowther's claim that he had never agreed to pay expenses to John Wordsworth, dominated their lives for the next twenty years, and would be resolved only by Lowther's successor.

Although the children's life in Cockermouth ended in grief, William's memories of his time there were uniformly happy. During these early years, William developed a cherished bond with his sister, and a love of the Cumbrian countryside – both providing him with a lifelong source of inspiration.

'Oh! Pleasant, pleasant were the days,
The time, when in our childish plays,
My sister Emmeline and I
Together chased the butterfly.'
TO A BUTTERFLY